Nightingale

Nightingale
Paisley Rekdal

COPPER CANYON PRESS
PORT TOWNSEND, WASHINGTON

Cover art: Sara VanDerBeek, *White Nude,* 2013. Courtesy of the artist and Metro Pictures, New York.

Copper Canyon Press is in residence at Fort Worden State Park in Port Townsend, Washington, under the auspices of Centrum. Centrum is a gathering place for artists and creative thinkers from around the world, students of all ages and backgrounds, and audiences seeking extraordinary cultural enrichment.

LIBRARY OF CONGRESS CATALOGING-IN-PUBLICATION DATA

Names: Rekdal, Paisley, author.
Title: Nightingale / Paisley Rekdal.
Description: Port Townsend, Washington : Copper Canyon Press, [2019]
Identifiers: LCCN 2018048966 | ISBN 9781556595677 (pbk. : alk. paper)
Classification: LCC PS3568.E54 A6 2019 | DDC 811/.54—dc23
LC record available at https://lccn.loc.gov/2018048966

98765432 FIRST PRINTING

COPPER CANYON PRESS
Post Office Box 271
Port Townsend, Washington 98368
www.coppercanyonpress.org

Academy of American Poets: "The Cry," "Psalm"; *Agni*, "Four Marys"; *The American Poetry Review*: "Nightingale: A Gloss"; *Fairy Tale Review*: "Psyche"; *Michigan Quarterly Review*: "Gokstadt/Ganymede"; *Narrative*: "Io," "The Olive Tree at Vouve," "Philomela," "Telling the Wasps," "Tiresias"; *New England Review*: "Horn of Plenty"; *Ploughshares*: "Astyanax"; *Poetry*: "Driving to Santa Fe," "The Wolves"; *PRISM International*: "Knitted Thylacine"; *Tin House*: "Marsyas," "Pasiphaë"; *Willow Springs*: "Pear," "Pythagorean."

"Nightingale: A Gloss," "Philomela," and "Quiver" were reprinted in *Philomela*, a chapbook published by Floodgate (2018). Thanks to Andrew McFadyen-Ketchum and all the editors at Floodgate.

"Marsyas" was reprinted in *Metamorphic: 21st Century Poets Respond to Ovid*. Much gratitude to the editors, Nessa O'Mahony and Paul Munden.

"Philomela" appeared in *Best American Poetry 2018*, edited by Dana Gioia. "Four Marys" will appear in *Best American Poetry 2019*, edited by Major Jackson. Sincere thanks to the editors, David Lehman, Dana Gioia, and Major Jackson.

Finally, boundless thanks to the Civitella Ranieri Foundation for a fellowship, and to Dana Prescott for her remarkable lectures on Piero della Francesca: "Four Marys" is for her. "Quiver" is a response/homage to Carl Phillips's "As from a Quiver of Arrows." "Pear" is a reimagining of Susan Stewart's "Apple." "Io" takes some details from Christina Crosby's *A Body, Undone*. Thanks to the University of Utah for support and for the gift of time. Thanks to Lisa Bickmore, Kimberly Johnson, Natasha Sajé, Susan Sample, and Jennifer Tonge. Special thanks to Sass Brown and Melanie Rae Thon for always being willing, generous, and brilliant readers. Thanks to the editorial vision and support of Michael Wiegers, and to the fantastic team at Copper Canyon Press. And thanks, ever and always, to Sean.

In memory of Gregory Beckelhymer

The substance is not chaunged, nor altered,
But th' only forme and outward fashion;
For every substance is conditioned
To change her hew, and sundry forms to don
                    Edmund Spenser, *The Faerie Queene,* bk. 3, canto 6

Why do you remove me from myself?
                    Ovid, *The Metamorphoses,* 6.385

Contents

Nightingale

I

Psalm

Too soon, perhaps, for fruit. And the broad branches,
ice-sheathed early, may bear none. But still my neighbor
waits, with her ladder and sack, for something to break.
A gold, a lengthening of light. For the greens to burst
into something not unlike flame: the pale fruit
blushing over weeks through the furred cleft creases:
a freckling of blood. Then the hot, sweet scent
of August rot, drawing wasps and birds and children
through the month. So much abundance, and the only cost
waiting. Looking at the tree, I almost expect the sound of bells,
a stone church, sheep in flocks. But no sound of bells,
no clarion call. The church is far down in the valley.
This tree should be an ancient, revered thing placed
at the heart of a temple. Instead, it is on a common
lot, beside a road, apartment buildings, a dog
sleeping in its yard. My neighbor has come here
neither as master nor supplicant. She simply plans
to fill a plastic sack with whatever she can take:
the sweet meat giving under the press of a thumb,
covering what is its true fruit: the little pit, hard
and almond-brown, that I've scooped out,
palmed, and planted to no avail. A better gardener
could make demands of such a seed, could train a tree
for what desire anticipates. But here the tree grows
only for itself. And if it bears no fruit for the killing
frost, or if it flowers late because of a too-warm winter,
what debt am I owed? At whose feet should I lay
disappointment? Delight no more comforting
nor wounding than hunger. The tree traffics
in a singular astonishment, its gold tongues
lolling out a song so rich and sweet, the notes
are left to rot upon the pavement. Is this the only religion
left to us? Not one only of mortification or desire,

not one of suffering, succor, not even of pleasure.
The juice of summer coils in the cells. It is a faith
that may not come to more than waiting.
To insist on pleasure alone is a mark
of childishness. To believe only in denial
the fool's prerogative. You hunger
because you hunger. And the tree calls to this.
But the fruit is real. I have eaten it. Have plucked
and washed and cut the weight, and stewed it
with sugar and lemon peel until the gold
ran rich and thick into jars. I have spooned it
over bread and meat. I have sucked it
from my husband's fingers. I have watched it sour
in its pots until a mist of green bubbled up
for a crust. I have gathered and failed it, as the tree
for me both ripens and fallows. But now, it is perhaps
too soon for fruit. The winter this year was hard,
the air full of smokes, and do I know if spring
reached the valley in time? Who planted this tree?
How long has it stood here? How many more years
can such a thing remain? My neighbor reaches a hand
up into the branches, palm cupped, weighing
the leaf knots. She is looking to see
what instincts, what weathers still grow here.
She snakes her hand through the greening branches.
Up from the valley come the golden tongues of bells.

Knitted Thylacine

Some still claim they are
alive, though the last-known sighting
was in 1930, their skins so rare, London's
zoology museum has only one

knitted replica for evidence, its fecal blooms
of stripes laddering a tan backside: four-teated,
pouchless; belly a dirt-streaked cream stretched
like a child's sweater atop a hoop
of willow switches.

         You can make one
from a pattern you can buy, knitting
its spotted pelt on size 2 and 4 needles, which are

quite small, circular: you have to slit the shape in two
when finished, the way my grandmother did,

slicing my father's sweaters
through the sternum, sewing back the deckle edge
of each honeycomb and cable, as the farmers

in Tasmania taught themselves to do, lost
in the colonies of a world no white woman
would enter, and so began

to think like women, sitting before the same fire, knitting
socks and scarves and sweaters
until this work turned from necessity

to art. The first goal with knitting
is utility, and so I'm moved by the strangeness
of these yarn-pelts'

burrs and slubs, the mohair tufts
thin as a kitten's undercoat, though you can't knit
the cough-like bark, the shining teeth;
you can't knit the jaw

that unhinges like a book
with a broken spine. The knitted skins
are smaller than their wiry

counterparts, delicate, soft
as the wives the farmers dreamed of, sick of work
their fathers would have said

made them soft, waiting for wives to come and make them
grow rough beards again and trim their nails
so as not to wound the thin

pink lips their fingers opened; though perhaps
for themselves they'd already kept
nails short, beards long, loving

how wet each other's mouths felt beneath
such bristles, each like a slick surprise: the buttery sex
cut out of the sea urchin, perhaps, a toy they made

from lumps of clay and rusted sewing needles
and slipped to a friend as a secret gift, *look*

what I have fashioned for you, the figure
conjuring forth alternately the spines
of hedgehogs, porcupines, the teeth

of the little cat-shaped devil that lives
in the bush and cries and cries

like the mating cats that used to draw
my teenaged father onto the porch,
swinging his flashlight into the dark

until he saw two green sets of eyes,
and shot at them with the gun his father left him.

Then he would take his spoils back down to the house where,
for curiosity's sake, he skinned them:
slicing the pelts up through the belly, soaking the remnants

in formaldehyde, trying
to get the shape of the animals just right
on his mother's table, knowing

what they should look like but unable
to duplicate it, not even knowing
what their last expression should be, that of pain

or of desire, for they'd died in both, as his mother
sat in the dark with a farmer
my father had to call uncle.

                  While an ocean away men sat
in their strained circles and pulled
one strand of yarn through the back loop
of another, trying to approximate

their sisters' stitches, sending samples in their letters
home, telling their mothers, *I am different now;*
telling their sweethearts, *I am changed,*

but keeping secret their stories
of a tiger that would steal your soul
if it found you, which is why

they called it a devil, for the way
it slept under the porch; for the way it would cry,
sounding like a lover, a brother, a friend, a mother,

sounding like an ache that can never be satisfied: how
could they say they'd never heard it, these men
knitting and knitting the same dream over?

Of course they heard the cry. It broke them in pieces.
And when they woke,
they slipped out of bed, gathered their lights,

and rushed into the dark to seize it.

The Cry

A man can cry, all night, your back
shaking against me as your mother
sleeps, hooked to the drip
to clear her kidneys from their muck
of sleeping pills. Each one white
as the snapper's belly I once watched a man
gut by the ice bins in his truck, its last
bubbling grunt cleaved in two
with a knife. The way my uncle's rabbit
growled in its cage, screamed
so like a child that when I woke the night
a fox chewed through the wires
to reach it, I thought it was my own voice
frozen in the yard. And then the fox,
trapped later by a neighbor, which thrashed
and barked as did the crows
that came for its eyes: the sound
of one animal's pain setting off a chain
in so many others, until each cry dissolves
into the next grown louder.
Even if I were blind
I would know night by the noise it made:
our groaning bed, the mewling
staircase, drapes that scrape
against glass panes behind which
stars rise, blue and silent.
But not even the stars
are silent: their pale waves
keen through space, echoing the dark
the way my father's disappointment
sags at my cheek, and his brother's angers
whiten his temple. And these
are your mother's shoulders shaking

in my arms tonight, her thin breath
that drags at our window where
coyotes cry: one calling to the next
calling to the next, their tender throats
tipped back to the sky.

Four Marys

Madonna del Parto, ca. 1460, Piero della Francesca

Are the drapes drawn open or being closed?
Each of the heavy, velvet wings is clasped
in the hands of a little angel, a little man really,
in shades of plum and mint green that frame
the birthing tent's opening for a girl
who retreats into or emerges from the dark.
It isn't clear: the perspective is such
that if I cover the painting's
top half with a hand, Mary steps forward;
if I cover the lower, she shrinks back,
her blue bodice split at the bulging seams
to show the pear-white cut of her linen shift,
the great weight of the child she is about to bear
and later bury. And even if I didn't believe
the child would rise again, I would believe the artist
had seen such fear paint a girl's face
when the eldest women in the village
were called for help, and fresh straw brought in
if there wasn't a bed, and hot water, and rose oil to rub
over the hips, and vinegar and sugar water
to drink, and hog's gut and a thick needle
to sew her up with later. Even if I did not believe
in Mary's joy, I would believe in her pain, the quick flick
of her thoughts turning to the sister, or the cousin,
or to her own mother who'd died giving birth,
the baby, too, not making it, for the birth
was in winter: ice so clogged the village's
deep ruts that the midwife's cart slipped
into the soak dike, splitting the wood wheel
in two, and by the time the woman could walk
the steep hill up to the villa, the mother had torn,

and in the rush to save her, no one worked
quick enough to cut the cord wrapped
around the baby's throat. Or the baby came out
strong and fine, but died two years later
when it stumbled into a fire, or was bitten by a rat
and sickened and starved, or caught the fever
that spread through town when all the animals
were stabled inside the houses for winter.
So many people died, so many people
were supposed to die, it's hard to conceive
of how the mothers survived their grief,
and how they named their next, living baby
after the dead one because the name, at least,
was good. It's hard to know whether I should read
the deepest grief or resignation or both in the line
from Mary Shelley's 1818 notebook, the year
her daughter, Clara, died, two weeks
after Mary had given birth to her. *Woke this morning.*
Found my baby dead, all the little black scratching pen
could add to paper, and the rest was blank,
and then there were months, and then
there was *Frankenstein.* Piero della Francesca
painted an embroidery of pomegranates
into Mary's birthing tent, symbol of fruitfulness
and the underworld, of a mother's grief
and of her rage to get her child back, the daughter
both dead and alive to her, as Mary knows her own child
is both dead and alive to us. A winter fruit
for the winter birth of a rich woman
whose house wanted to ward off a grueling
delivery, and so whose midwife would feed her
pomegranate seeds to sustain her, a fruit
the midwife herself would eat only once, as payment
from the duke for the son she finally ushered
into the world for him. Such a strange, leathery

skin, though the color was bright
as blood on fresh linen, and who could have expected
those glistening cells packed inside, wet prisms
in the ruby eye of a ruby insect, or the heart
of a god who takes what he wants
and never gives it back. The midwife took the fruit home
and split it with her husband and tried not to think
of the bed of the girl she'd just left, its stains
that looked almost black in the dawn light,
and how the girl's skin had turned bluish, the fragile spring
she'd require to spend alone in bed away from the duke
and healing. How can Mary not look
downcast before these curtains that threaten
to close on her, to open? *I have no doubt*
of seeing the animal today, Mary Wollstonecraft
Godwin, Mary Shelley's mother, wrote,
meaning birth, meaning Mary, the little animal
she never saw grow up, because Wollstonecraft
died of an infection days after giving birth.
But before that was told she could not nurse
her infant daughter for fear the corruption
would spread through her milk, though she stayed
at Mary's bedside the final three days of her life.
And Godwin stayed beside her, who, because he loved
his wife, believed her genius could survive
any truth, and so published a memoir later
detailing everything: Wollstonecraft's affairs,
her daughter's illegitimacy, her attempts at suicide—so that
in 1798 the index of the *Anti-Jacobin Review* would publish,
under the heading "Prostitution," *See Mary*
Wollstonecraft. Two towns over from his Madonna,
in a church in Arezzo, Piero della Francesca
painted a fresco of Mary Magdalene, her curled hair wet
with the tears she used to bathe Christ's feet,
her body a swollen green swathe of dress, the red cape

folded to accentuate the pendulous belly
and thick thigh, the Magdalene bristling
between arch columns that frame her, one
painted slightly forward, the other behind
her body, so that we do not know in which direction
Mary is headed, nor what she is, really,
her almond eyes glittering out at us, her halo chipped,
over centuries, away. It is wonderful
when time accentuates something of the truth
already within us: the frank look, the unabashed
leg with which the woman kicks off the covers from the bed
of the man to whom she is not married; the neat,
round muscle of his shoulder pressed against hers
in the dark, his body over and over coming alive
under her hands, a dream or a nightmare
Mary Shelley once had of Clara.
All this time, she told her husband, their daughter
had not been dead at all, only cold, the little body frozen
and waiting to be attended to. *And so we rubbed
it before the fire, and now it lives,* she told
Shelley in the conversation recorded
in her journal, and cried awhile, and went to bed.
Then woke again the next morning, and remembered.
The midwife, walking back down from the villa
three summers later, having attended the birth
of the duke's new, less delicate wife, hums a song
to herself that she hummed to the baby
she just left, a girl this time, no pomegranates
for payment; a girl who will, if lucky, inherit
her mother's strength and her plainness, both traits
the midwife believes might protect her from
and in the birthing bed. She'll grow up,
the midwife thinks, and marry, and have children
herself, some less or more like her, sons
with obdurate natures, perhaps, or a daughter

who inherits her curly hair, perhaps the sturdy thighs
of a woman like this shopkeeper kneeling now by a store
in the Piazza Grande to retrieve a shower of euros
from someone's coin purse. The woman stands, straightens,
and I see her mouth thin to a not unpleasant line
as she looks out at me, calculating, perhaps,
the time until lunch as she tugs at the waist
of her linen pants. The yellow pleats sag, slack
at her belly. The weight from a pregnancy
she never lost, perhaps, or the thickening
that comes to anyone, in the later part of life.

Psyche

The photos of the boy were taken first
          in play, but when one
     emerged in the darkroom's

bath of her son's back stained
          in palladium whip-
     stripes like blood, she began

to pose him: the red scarf noosed
          at his collar's
     hollow, thin neck bent, one

red thread wrapped
          in a cut's lash
     brightening his throat. *Ghastly,*

she'd tell anyone
          who looked, thinking
     if she could photograph

such fears they wouldn't
          come true. And so she had
     her son submerge himself

as if drowning
          in the bath, stand
     by the forest's edge at dusk, his small

shape lost among the white
          ash branches. No more,
     she told herself, though more

always came to her: the imagination
          for pain, it seemed,
     was endless. *Make me*

scared, she commanded
 her son, and he did: this boy,
 skirting some tragedy

she sensed inscribed
 for them both, whose skin
 she'd stroked, nibbling

the tears off his baby
 cheeks, and once—
 kissing the crown of his head

still bathed in birth-blood—
 almost tasted.
 Had she always contained

such menace? In the day,
 her boy was gorgeous,
 joyful. But the camera's

eye caught something
 else: the plum bruise blooming
 from a spider bite, his teenage

legs stripped, spread bare
 on the carpet. How
 those plush scarlets flushed

against his kneecaps. She loved
 that photo best
 of all, the unflinching bones

her camera found, his big feet splayed
 as if the ankles
 had been broken. How

could she have known his illness
                    lurked inside except
          her camera found it, reached

across time to devour
                    the just-budded
          calf muscles, the long,

lean tendons of his legs?
                    The sweet spot,
          she called her work

when light hit her son
                    just right. *Magic,*
          her son once said.

He does not call it magic now.

The Wolves

It was the week of asking. Asking
to watch her eat. Asking if she understood
the doctors' questions. Asking her
to explain the difference again between
wanting to die right now
and dying later.
The tumor making certain answers
unquestionable. I watched her point
to the incense dish from which
someone swept all the ashes up. Asking
if she recognized us. Because that
is what the living want: thinking
it is a sign we have been loved.
But the answer was a summer
drive, a mountain, piles of leaves beneath which
a wolf slept, suckling her pups.
Some deaths are good
and it makes them hard to grieve.
She was, at times, in great pain. We wanted her
to die, too. That was important. But first
we wanted her to remember.
From the bed, a finger pressed
into its pile of leaves. Gray haunch,
unmovable ashes. *I didn't want to disturb
their tableau,* she told us. And drifted off. And
we did not know the meaning behind this.
The wolves must have looked so comfortable
to her: wordless and in this wordlessness
perfect. Did she want to go there, too.
I could point to the image and say, my father
must be in there, my uncle. Or, the wolf
is you, you are still the mother,
as if necessary to name that self

at the end of its world. An animal cry,
memory. That was our selfishness.
As death was hers. She insisted upon it.
And why not. *It was good for me*
to get a chance to know you,
she said, who had known me
my entire life. Then the pills, a small
handful, crushed into juice.
She was happy then. We all were. Or
said we were. What
is the difference now.

Tiresias

She knew, before her daughter did,
that they would need a different body.
And so she saved up for the surgeries,
as soon as her daughter began to cup
her urine in a plastic funnel to pee
the way she'd seen her father do,
before he died. As soon as she'd begun
to pluck her lashes out at school, as soon
as she'd had to buy a dress suit
from the boys' store to placate her daughter
into attending a family wedding. It wasn't coyness
that had made her daughter want to hide
the breasts that swelled, causing the girl
at night to cry. And if she herself cried
to find locks of her daughter's shorn
brown hair curled under the bathroom sink,
she excused these tears by saying,
*I'm only sorry you never asked
for help,* to hide the fact it was
not lack of usefulness but loss
which daily terrified her. *She looks
like you,* friends said to compliment
their closeness, and over the years
she wondered at those similarities:
the strong jaw and slim hips inherited
from her own father; her full breasts thin now,
slack from the weight she'd lost (*Stress,*
her therapist had warned her), aware
of the looks the two of them generated
in the grocery store, at the movie theater.
Boy or girl, her child would always be
attractive, she knew, relieved to think at least
he'd be, in that strange way of beauty,

anonymous. Though anonymity was never
what her daughter wanted. It is not
what she wants, either, pulling back
the sagging lids of her eyes, imagining
the breast lift, tummy tuck: she could
have gotten them all, lying next to her daughter
in matching hospital gowns, both of them
working to unearth something beautiful
from this flesh that, daily, betrayed them.
And now, after her diagnosis, she wonders
why she never asked. To remove
the breasts entirely, cut out the slick
dark bag of womb, stitch out from fat
and labia some length of skin
she'd learn to call a penis—
She imagines standing, naked,
before her child, the two of them
still the spitting image of each other: mirrors
to the last, broken and remade
in the same places. *How could anyone
love me,* her daughter once had asked,
if I'm not entirely myself? And though
she'd never believed love
could occur only in some specific
version of a body, now, struggling not
to despise her sickened flesh, to remember
some idea of herself that once felt
capable of desire, she thinks her child
was right. Every day, she pretends
to understand what is happening
to her body, what has happened
to her daughter, but there is no understanding
this. Each of them contains a separate
mesh and web of cells, connections
utterly unlike the other's, something

she both mourns and is, oddly,
grateful for: their differences now
as palpable, as powerful as the chromosome
neither of them can fake. Years ago,
before they wheeled her daughter
into her first surgery, she tried to picture
which of her brothers her child
would emerge resembling, what kind of son
he'd be, what kind of mother
he would want, and how she could perform
that, over and over, to give her son the love
his real body craved. In all those years since,
had she ever succeeded? *You're mother
and father to me,* her son tells her now,
joking on the phone, calling
to ask after her latest biopsy, which he hopes
once more will be benign. He calls every Friday
from the TV station where he works, proud
of his job, his new life, his large apartment
by the bay. He's thoughtful,
she thinks; he smiles more easily.
He speaks in low, clipped tones that don't sound
entirely like her daughter's. Or don't sound entirely
unlike them either. *I'm fine,* she lies
to assure him now. *Everything's the same.*
Jamie, her son has named himself. After his mother's
Scottish grandfather.

Horn of Plenty

Would you do what this artist did? The one
who bought fresh goat's blood to pour
over the cornucopia he sculpted in protest
of the war, its dark mouth large enough
for a yearling kid to sleep in, head tucked
between the glossy hooves: for in his mind
the animal was clean, the farm a bright,
mechanical place where anyone could buy
clear bags of meat and blood. But the farm
he found was poor, its owner's health
failing, and so the artist, chagrined
perhaps by his ambitions, watched
as the farmer trudged into a muddy copse
with a pail to pull two thin animals into his barn.
Then he locked his knees around the smallest
one's neck, its hips and triangular head
twisting in his grip, so he levered the blade
clumsily across the goat's gullet, forced now to saw
through the tough neck muscles, the animal's head
violently shaking *no, no, no* until the head
pulled free and was thrown upon the ground.
Then the farmer knelt down and punched his knife
through the belly to pull out viscera, fresh
and hot, the dark blood pumping into his pail
as the other goat backed up against the far wall, screaming—

Would you have chosen to stop?
Or would you have continued, knowing
you wanted the blood because of the horn: symbol
both of plenty and of suffering, because it was a goat
who nursed the god who snapped this horn off
once in play? And blessed it later to be
forgiven. That the horn recalled the grain

of the once-fertile nation your country has invaded:
a country from which your government says
it can't withdraw, its fields and infrastructure
depleted by years of drought and war.
The goat is ancient, milky-eyed. She's half-blind,
though she can smell what's happened
to her companion: the whole barn is thick with the death
that will now be hers. Would you keep on going?
Does the first animal's suffering only make sense
if you complete your art, finish the sculpture in a way
the war will never be finished, the great horn
clotted with blood and displayed
in the foyer of the museum that commissioned it?
The show will be titled after a line from *The Iliad:*
Freighted with Dark Pains, a description of the arrow
shot by one soldier into the heart of another.
The curators chose the title for the beauty
of that line, perhaps for its suggestion
that the body giving and the body receiving pain
were equally blameless: only the arrow
delivers sorrow, only the arrow aches
as it rips through skin and muscle into the tender
flank of the animal you are even now
stroking in your arms. How can you not
hush and cluck at her, soothing this goat
the way you'd soothe the fears of anyone
you loved, bending down to gather her body
tightly against your own,
because the animal is old, already dying,
because you're tired of watching
such frantic suffering, and because
it is not your knife carrying the pain.

Astyanax

They laughed, at first, at his shrieks
seeing the face his father wore: a horse-head
mask unearthed from the closet
where he kept his army uniform, the white
rubber face with real hair for a mane
under which his father's shoulders bulged.
His father's broad hands tossed the boy
onto his back, and he clung to him, this child
who'd never before seen an animal
like his father, though they'd read him stories
of ponies and gentle cart horses, bulls
in a field eating flowers, once a bugling buck
with its brace of horns.
Nothing like this. The teacup nostrils
flamed with blood, the pink lips cracked back
into a sneer. It filled the air
with muffled cries, the long mane dark
as his mother's hair, and just as fine, as if
he'd shorn it from her: this thing
racing with him now to the kitchen where
it could kick the whole
house down, jump the fence, tear
off with him across oceans.
The white skin sagged at the neck.
Perhaps, if they took this face off, his father
would return and he could stop crying,
though when the mask came off
the boy did not stop crying: there were
powdery creases now in his father's face,
and his skin smelled bitter, burning.
His father tossed the mask aside
and pressed his son's face into his neck.
And still the boy did not stop crying, could not stop

seeing that wild, gray face even in sleep, and so woke
crying again the next morning, regardless
of his mother's songs, his father's smiles,
regardless of how his parents tried
to make a joke of it. How they laughed
and laughed, who loved him
and could not console him.

Io

Of course, everyone wondered about the sex:
how Jane and she were handling it
since the bike accident last May that left her
quadriplegic. Perhaps some had always
wondered: Jane, the pretty teacher
who'd left her husband for her; she, the knob-
kneed, almond-eyed pastry chef who biked
each day to the café where she worked,
swinging her ten-speed over a shoulder *just
like a boy,* Jane said, delighting
in this strength, though now she couldn't swing
a cat over her shoulder. Her arms
she can barely lift past her sides, her legs
are both there and gone, the spinal cord severed
from when the car behind her clipped
a tire, sending her face-first
into the pavement. Having learned
she'd never walk again, her own
thoughts soon gravitated to sex: nights
with Jane curled on the living room futon
they used as a couch until they gave up
all pretense and left the bed spread
open to let them move more easily
from talking to making love, the burn
of sex's ache still vivid in her fingers, she
stunned by the fact it is not numbness now
but total feeling that defines her. Her body
is no longer the source of pleasure
but constant pain, a dim prickling
in thighs and feet, phantom
throbbings up through her pelvis,
though it is the pleasure that she mourns
most clearly: that slight dampness

to her scalp after a run, or the tightening
muscles in her legs as she stood
and pushed against the bike pedals.
She'd never known how much her body
was meant for this, trapped
inside these shrinking muscles that at times
make her feel as if she were two
women: one confined to bed
or chair, the other with her hands
still cupping Jane's breasts. She remembers
once being read a story about a girl
taken by a god who, to shield her
from his wife's jealousy, changed her
into a cow. The tale was meant first either
as a moral or a comedy, she can't
be sure, only that the girl
never stopped hating her broad,
silk flanks, her viscous nose, the head
double-weighted down with horns.
Even her gentle, chime-like lowing
only masked her human cries: a hunger
she could never satisfy with grass.
The horror, she tries to explain to Jane, is not
that she has changed but that she can't change
entirely. Memory makes some part of her stay
always the same, and when she looks at Jane
reading on the futon refolded back into a couch,
she cries. Jane, to comfort her, insists
her desire for her is exactly the same, but it cannot be
the same desire. It is an old desire locked
inside a new body, one of clumsy,
twisted fingers, shriveled legs,
bedsores. Even Jane is not Jane anymore
to her, her skin papery where once
she felt plush; no more sandpaper

rasp to the armpits, legs; she even tastes
less musky, as if her very tongue
has dulled. Jane tells her she's become
more soulful, considerate, as if to make
her differences some new reward, though
this only enrages her. Better
that one day she wakes to find
all memory gone, so that she might inhabit
this new body perfectly, wanting
what she's always wanted: a whole self
without any sense of loss, even as she knows
loss would always have come for her.
It was built into the equation of any body:
the waning mind, waning desire, the flicker
of a life just fading into the distance. *What
are you reaching for, honey?* Jane asks now
as she shifts slightly in her chair. And holds out
a glass of water to her twitching fingers,
which she takes, quietly, as if all along this
was what she'd been reaching for.

II

Philomela

Because her grandmother loved
the arts, her father said, she'd willed
the money to a distant cousin
working as a sculptor. A decision
made the month before she'd died
from cancer, which the young woman
cannot now believe was due
only to a brain tumor, having endured
the last, deliberate ways her grandmother asked
why she'd never married.
The cousin who inherited the money
showed her sculptures in a converted barn,
the only space large enough to contain
the seething shapes that seemed to flame
up from their pedestals
in precarious arcs. An audacity
of engineering the young woman
tried not to see as a reproach
when, curious, she visited:
how the sculptures made her feel
too earthbound, solid. At the gallery,
she stared a long while at what she thought
was a tree blasted by lightning,
but the more she looked, the more clearly
shapes emerged. There
were a man's hands gripping a slender figure
by the waist, the thin body writhing,
frozen in his arms. It was
a girl, she saw, with shredded
bark for breasts and dark, charred wood
for legs, as if the limbs had been snatched
from a fire while burning.
Her twig hands raked

her captor's face. The young woman
could read no emotion on it,
however: the plank face
had been scraped clean; all the fear
and anger burned instead inside
their twisting bodies: she could see
the two there stuck at a point
of perfect hatred for each other: she
for his attack, he for her resistance,
perhaps the beauty he could not
stand in her, as her last date in college
had hissed, "You think
you're so fucking pretty," spitting it
into her face so that she'd had to turn
her cheek to wipe it, which was when
he'd grabbed her arm, pinning her—

Was this why her cousin had been chosen, to make
what she'd had no words for?
Persephone, the piece she stood
amazed before had been titled: the last,
perhaps unconscious gift of her grandmother.
"For your wedding," she'd said
during her last week, pointing
to her own open palm in which
nothing rested. Perhaps
her grandmother had imagined
a gold ring there. Perhaps a string
of thick pink pearls. The young woman
drove home from the gallery, took a shower,
and did not tell anyone that day
what it was she'd seen. A month later,
in the mail, a package came
from her father: her grandmother's Singer
sewing machine, its antique brass wheel
scrubbed of gold, the wooden handle

glossy with vines of mother-of-pearl.
It was lovely, and for a moment
she considered sewing a quilt with it,
onto which she might embroider
shooting stars in reds and saffron, the figure
of a child, perhaps, or of a man
by a house's courtyard, his hat
in his hands, his broad body
naked, harmless.

How much thread would that take
to make? she wondered. And considered it
a long while before packing up
the machine again, sliding it back
into its wood crate and high up onto a shelf
of her bedroom closet. The place she kept
some books, old clothes, and college papers,
where she told herself it could wait.

Nightingale: A Gloss

> Nay, then I'll stop your mouth.
> Shakespeare, *Titus Andronicus,* II, iii

Language is the first site of loss and our first defense against it. Which is why after Philomela's brother-in-law, Tereus, rapes her, he cuts out her tongue and tosses it, the bloody stump writhing at her feet.

*

In my poem "Philomela," I leave out this mutilation. Strike out Philomela's sister, Procne, who learns of her sister's rape from the tapestry Philomela weaves. Cut the death of Itys, Procne's son, whom the sisters dismember and boil for punishment, Philomela, mute but grinning, tossing the boy's head at his father. No metamorphosis of Philomela and Procne into nightingale and swallow, Tereus shrunk into the hoopoe that pursues them. Such details would be unimaginable, I think. Not because a contemporary reader can't imagine them, but because the details are now too grotesque for her to want to.

*

Ovid makes the trio's transformation occur at the instant syntax shifts from the conditional to the imperfect. "[The girls] went flying…/ [as] if they were on wings. They were on wings!" he writes. The difference between simile and metaphor. The second the mouth conceives it, the imagination turns it into the real.
The Metamorphoses, 6.669–670

*

I'm writing "Philomela" at an artists' colony where I go for daily runs. Sometimes a man in a car will pace me; sometimes a man on his bike will circle back to get another look. Sometimes the men who pass me say nothing.

Around this residency are woods in which, the staff informs us, we can walk. It is beautiful here, and there are olive groves. I do not walk by myself in the woods.

*

It's 1992 and I'm hiking near Loch Ness. It's after breakfast: I've spent the morning alone in a stand of gold aspen that circles the lake. When the three men find me, the smell of beer and whiskey thick on their clothes, bait boxes and fishing rods in hand, I have just sat down with a book. The men are red-eyed, gruff. The first two nod as they pass me: it is the third who walks back. He has lank, gingery hair and black spots in his teeth.

Hello, he says when he reaches me.

*

Nightingale: OE *nihtegala, niht + galan*, small, reddish-brown migratory bird celebrated for its sweet night song during the breeding season. In Dutch, a frog.
Virgil, *The Georgics,* Book IV:
>[A]s mourning beneath the poplar shade the nightingale
>laments her lost brood... she sobs
>nightlong, and on a branch perched her doleful song
>renews—
Shelley, *A Defence of Poetry:* "A poet is a nightingale who sits in darkness, and sings to cheer its solitude with sweet sounds; his auditors are as men entranced by the melody of an unseen musician."

*

Are you an American? he asks. I always wanted to kiss an American.

*

Female nightingales do not sing. Only the male sings, as Tereus does, attempting to woo Philomela with words. "Love made him eloquent," Ovid writes, suggesting that Tereus's language is aroused by Philomela's silence.

What space is a woman? "[S]ome Pallas in place which furthered my in-uention. For I am in that point of Ouid his opinion, that, *Si cupiat sponte disertus erit.*" (Desire makes a man spontaneously eloquent.) A palace of pleasure arousing both erotic and narrative desires.
George Pettie, *A Petite Pallace of Pettie his Pleasure,* 1576.

*

Just a kiss, he says, dropping his tackle box, and I know I should run. He grabs my head, and I am already clawing at his neck, terrified for myself but also terrified of hurting him. Hurting him will make it worse for me. He hisses in my ear as I slap his hands, and now he's got his arms around me. I rear back, unbalancing myself, so that when I do the one thing I've been taught, which is to bring my right knee up hard into his groin, the blow is too weak.

That didn't work, I stammer, as my leg grazes the inside of his thigh.

It never does, he replies. And now he has me on the ground.

*

Philomel, Philomela: ME, from Greek *philo* + *melos*, song, a nightingale. Matthew Arnold, "Philomela":

How thick the bursts come crowding through the leaves!
   Again—thou hearest!
   Eternal passion!
   Eternal pain!

*

I do not use my voice. Two other men are ahead of us in the woods: I have no idea what they will do if called back, where their allegiances will lie. As if these were rules agreed upon, he doesn't shout either. In retro-spect, his silence suggests that his friends might have taken my side. But at that moment, the two of us cajole and beg and threaten in hisses. The whole attack is conducted in silence.

Ovid says it is imagination that makes possible this sudden turn toward violence: Tereus "sees beyond what he sees," an idea embroidered on by later writers. "[H]ee seemed to see her stand apparently before him (only a stronge imagination assurynge him that it was shee) which sight sunk so deeply into his heart and brought him such excessiue delight, that hee presently awaked, and missing the partie that procured him such pleasure, his ioy was turned to anoy," writes George Pettie in his rewriting of the myth. To see past what we know into what we desire, to put that desire into language. And by performing that, to enact in the reader a similar performance. The art is not complete until we imagine the outcome for ourselves.

A Petite Pallace of Pettie his Pleasure
The Metamorphoses, 6.453–482

*

My hands are pushed up against his chest, his hands are in my pants, on my breasts. He says nothing, though he grimaces, his face close to my own as he leans to kiss me, so I whip my head away. I can feel the cold leaves against my cheek, the damp earth, can spy my book lying a few feet off. *Just let him*, something small, dry, miserable in me says. *Let him, and it will all be over.* But I don't. I keep my mouth shut, and I fight.

*

There is no scream after the tongue is cut, but would we hear a cry? Philomela screams only in the text, thus in our minds: in that, her body and our own do not communicate. We *cannot* hear her. We want to, but she exists only in our imagination: an absent body that exists in the past or an unforeseeable future. She begs for help we can never give. It is absurd to suggest we could. In that sense, she never needed a tongue to scream for help. She never had one.

K. Frances Lieder, "*Lights Out* and an Ethics of Spectatorship, or Can the Subaltern Scream?"

The rape isn't described in my poem "Philomela": it takes place offstage, recorded years after the event by the character who experienced it. I left out the rape, thinking to reject a reader's voyeurism. But the reader of myths knows what is left out: my silence, then, is not a revision but an invitation to imagine, to remember, this violence for yourself.

*

Procne, too, must imagine her sister's violation. Philomela's weaving thus becomes a muslin veil drawn over experience, both bringing her sister in and shutting her out.

*

And then his fingers are tearing inside me, his tongue filling my own mouth.

*

The woods are ruthless, dreadful, deaf, and dull;
There speak, and strike, brave boys, and take your turns;
There serve your lusts, shadow'd from heaven's eye,
And revel in Lavinia's treasury.
Titus Andronicus, II, i

*

He stops. He withdraws his hand from my pants, lets go my hair. I curl my legs up into my chest as he pushes himself, unsteadily, off me. That wasn't much, was it? he asks. He brushes leaves off his clothes.

*

When I try to explain what his teeth looked like, what his breath smelled like, the cold ridges of his nails as they clawed inside me, I know I am asking for something beyond the response of your own suffering, your awareness of my suffering. I don't care what you know or how you feel. I want to go back in time, to an eternal *before.* I want you to give me what no one can give me. Which is why, for many years, I have resisted speaking about it.

*

Tongue: OE *tunge* and Latin *lingua,* an organ of speech, a figure or representation of this organ; the faculty of speech. A voice, a vote, suffrage. To assail with words; to cut a tongue; to slit or shape a tongue in a plant for grafting. Giving great tongue: a cry made by hounds when they scent a fox.

*

"Will not my tongue be mute?" Tarquin wonders, at the thought of raping Lucretia. The momentary horror he experiences believing that the rape must mark him as well: a blot upon his face as well as language, violence carving its sin upon his own self. If she cannot go unmarked, he cannot either; the body giving tongue to its distress.
Shakespeare, *The Rape of Lucrece,* 227

*

It is not rape, and yet. Sexual violence has been historically difficult to articulate. Chaucer devoted much of the fifth book of *The Legend of Good Women,* in which he retells the myth of Philomela, to creating subcategories of words akin to rape: *ravine,* a rape linked with abduction; *robberie,* a rape occurring in the woods; *stelthe,* an attack cloaked in secrecy. We would not care to make such distinctions, but Chaucer's characters do. When Amans (Latin: "Loving") is asked whether he has committed the sin of ravine, he denies it, admitting only to the possibility of stelthe. It is important, he demands, to be specific. What happened to me feels like something that exists between words, a subcategory of expression for which there is no one easy expression.

Ravine: OF *raviner* and L. *rapinare,* to pillage, sweep down, to violently sweep away.

*

Raving: MF *resver*, to wander, to be delirious. "Raving" is applied to the Bacchantes or Maenads, whose name means "raving ones." Procne first appears in Ovid's tale dressed as the Bacchantes' queen, "in all the dress / of frenzy," spear over her shoulder, draped in vines and deer hide. Philomela, voiceless suffering, is visited by her sister, rage. A raping. A raving.
The Metamorphoses, 6.589–590

*

"Raving": at the heart of the story is madness, a word sonically, if not etymologically, attached to the word for rape. Raving is a contagion that spreads through imagination and desire. To the ancient writers, only raving breeds and explains female aggression. Agave, driven mad by Dionysus for her "unbridled tongue," doesn't know her son, Pentheus, spikes his head on a stake. Medea, to punish an unfaithful Jason, dismembers their children. To wound one is to wound the other, bodies linked by sperm and milk and blood. Don't infect me with your madness.
Euripides, *The Bacchae*, 1.438

*

If art is the eloquence left Philomela, what answer does it inspire? Pain speaks to pain. "Why should one make pretty speeches and the other be dumb?" Procne wonders, looking back and forth between Philomela's tapestry and her son. Itys's ability to speak throws Philomela's silence into loud relief, and though he says nothing in the myth, his flesh "keep[s] something of the spirit" alive. When Procne dismembers him, he "leap[s] in the boiling kettles… hisse[s] on the turning skewers." Pain, too, is a language. It raves in me with a diabolic tongue.
The Metamorphoses, 6.647–649
Czeslaw Milosz, "Language"

*

Rape is the dark seam of *The Metamorphoses*. To Ovid, a poet, perhaps the ultimate dehumanizing act would bring the body to a place beyond language. People in his versions of the myths often become animals, men and women "more cut off from words than a seal," as Robert Lowell wrote of one manic stint spent in McLean. To live cut off from words is to descend into the bodily, the irrational. It is, if words make law and government, to be outside political power. To make his (literate, male) audience understand such powerlessness, Ovid frames the rape from Philomela's point of view. He centers male agency within a silent female consciousness.

Lowell, "Waking in the Blue," 24

*

But if you stubbornly keep lying down in bed, dressed,
    You'll feel my hands by way of your torn dress:
In fact, if my anger should carry me further,
    You'll show wounded arms to your mother.

Propertius 2.15.17–20

Or Ovid features rape because it is a trope of Roman elegiac discourse. *Arma, amor, ira.* Either way, desire is scripted by violence.

*

Madness to insist upon narrative cohesion when the story is one of fragmentation, chaos. The story is one of raving. Philomela's descent is an unveiling of the animal heart at the world's center. The girl, running as if flying into the woods. The girl flying. Tereus crystallized in the body of a spike-crowned predator. If we become the thing that symbolizes us, it is not change then, but revelation.

*

[Tereus] was a passionate man, and all the Thracians
are quick at loving; a double fire
all too burned in him: his own passion and his nation's.

To Ovid, violence is brute, natural, indifferent; it wells up in men's blood,
a moral emptiness that obeys no rules because it understands none. In
The Metamorphoses, the truth of violence is that it might erupt at any
time: the void always threatens to yawn before us, and we struggle to
assemble words that will explain it. Only language, which orders time and
gives experience shape and meaning, might control how violence is expe-
rienced. It gives back agency. "There was no time ever / when she would
rather have had the use of her tongue, / the power to speak, to express
her full rejoicing," Ovid writes, after Philomela throws Itys's bloody head
at Tereus's feet. Language is made to contain our awareness of, even our
celebration in, suffering. The pain attending our pleasure. The pleasure we
take in another's pain.
The Metamorphoses, 6.460–462, 659–661

*

Here are the words describing Philomela's cut tongue: *immurmurat*
(murmurs), *palpitat* (quivers), *quaerit* (strives). Like a lover, the tongue
murmurs, it quivers, it strives for its mistress.
The Metamorphoses, 6.562–564

*

Positioning an implicitly male audience in the consciousness of a raving,
raped woman tilts the myth from one of identification to one of rejec-
tion. To portray Philomela's calls for justice within the frame of madness
reduces her moral justification for Tereus's punishment. It focuses the
reader's gaze back upon her mutilated body, her tortured mind, turning
our regard from one of empathy to spectacle.

*

Keats, in his copy of *Titus Andronicus,* a play that rewrites the myth of
Philomela, struck out with his pen several of the taunting lines spoken by

Demetrius and Chiron after they've raped Lavinia, sliced out her tongue, and cut off her hands. He drew his pen vigorously over their dialogue, mutilating their speech: violence overwriting violence.

*

MARCUS
Speak, gentle niece, what stern ungentle hands
Have lopp'd and hew'd and made thy body bare
Of her two branches, those sweet ornaments—

In Julie Taymor's *Titus*, Lavinia wears branches for hands, recalling Shakespeare's recurring metaphor: Lavinia's hands "tremble, like aspen-leaves, upon a lute"; Chiron, sneering, suggests her "stumps will let [her] play the scribe." Wood as scene of violation, wood as body, body as failed writing instrument. Lavinia's changes, too, are metonymic. *The girls run as if they are flying. They are flying!*
Titus Andronicus, II, iv

*

Branch: ME and F *branche*, a tree limb or stem, a child; also *fig.* a division, to strike out on a new path, to divide.
Hew: OE *heawan*, to strike forcefully, to cut, to shape, to slaughter.
Limb: OT *limo-*, organ or part of the body; **limb** (L, *limbus*), an edge or boundary of a surface.

*

Near an olive grove by the residency lives a bird that mimics human song. An opera singer stands there certain afternoons, dust in the tall grasses, heat bringing out the scent of lemon and jasmine. She sings into the field where the unseen bird nests, a tree branch swaying under its small body. The bird waits a beat after she finishes, then—matching her note for note—trills back. Try it yourself, she says, charmed by the idea of speaking across species. Perhaps a mating call. Perhaps a delineation of territory.

*

Keats returned often to the figure of the nightingale: a symbol common to the Romantic poets.

"Ode to a Nightingale":

> Still wouldst thou sing, and I have ears in vain—
>> To thy high requiem become a sod.

"The Eve of St Agnes":

> She clos'd the door, she panted, all akin
> To spirits of the air, and visions wide:
> No uttered syllable, or, woe betide!
> But to her heart, her heart was voluble,
> Paining with eloquence her balmy side;
> As though a tongueless nightingale should swell
> Her throat in vain, and die, heart-stifled, in her dell.

"La Belle Dame Sans Merci":

> And no birds sing.

I am most interested in his Philomela reference in "The Eve of St. Agnes." It is not only that his Madeline is like Philomela, voiceless while her body throbs with unspoken pain, but that Keats's Philomela, his nightingale, must die.

*

DEMETRIUS
~~So, now go tell, an if thy tongue can speak,~~
~~Who 'twas that cut thy tongue and ravish'd thee.~~
CHIRON
~~Write down thy mind, bewray thy meaning so,~~
~~An if thy stumps will let thee play the scribe.~~
DEMETRIUS
~~She hath no tongue to call, nor hands to wash;~~
~~And so let's leave her to her silent walks.~~

*

Is the metonym, finally, for Philomela art, or silence, or raving? Later poets' use of the nightingale suggests she is a poet able to sing about and against suffering, but Ovid never mentions song. Instead, he symbolizes Philomela and Procne by their murder of Itys: "And even so the red marks of the murder / stayed on their breasts; the feathers were blood-colored." What is our longing to hear Philomela's song but our own desire for retributive justice? Ovid's story is clear: the tongue that might give voice to reparation is mute beside the body's recounting of injury. Philomela's story, then, is meant to excite, to enrage.

The Metamorphoses, 6.672–673

*

Perhaps the greatest desire a victim of violence has is to look at that violence dispassionately in memory. But remembering, the heart pounds, the body floods with adrenaline, ready to tear back off into flight. For some, there is no smoothing chaos into memory. Poetry, with its suggestion that time and pain can be ordered through language, strains to constrain suffering. It suggests, but rarely achieves, the redress we desire. Language does not heal terror, and if it brings us closer to imagining the sufferer's experience, this too does not necessarily make us feel greater compassion but a desire for further sensation. If we cannot articulate pain beyond inspiring in the listener a need for revenge, we speak only of and to the body.

*

Philomela's first communication of pain is visual: as in a film, her tortures scroll action by action across her tapestry. Like a film, these images manipulate emotion: Philomela's pain cannot be relieved except through equivalent, mimetic actions that heighten the need for, but never achieve, the catharsis denied the original sufferer.

*

What if it is the form, not the content, of *The Metamorphoses* that is the terror? Each story unfolding into another, perpetually disrupting, thus delaying the ending? What if, because we came to listen, we are the reason the story keeps not ending? Why should Philomela sing, when our presence only increases her suffering?

*

Sufferance: ME *soffrance* and Latin *suffrer,* patient endurance; the suffering of pain, trouble, damage, wrong; sanction, consent, or acquiescence. **Suffer**: to cause pain; also, to endure pain.

*

That the branches of poetry are silence and sufferance.

*

In my poem "Philomela," the woman who has been raped inherits—years after her attack—an antique sewing machine from her grandmother. She imagines using this machine to sew a quilt on which she will embroider figures of the domestic life her grandmother ruefully noted she did not have: a house, a child, a man. But after a few minutes' contemplation, she boxes up the machine, slides it high up on a bedroom shelf. What is she communicating? Who would she be speaking to? She can always return to the quilt, she tells herself, but in the unwritten rest of the poem I imagine for her, she never will.

*

Not rape, I say, meaning certain body parts and not others were used, meaning I do not cede that last ignominy to him, will never name how I lay in the dirt and ground my screams back down into me. But what is the word for what I experienced after? What is the word for how I awoke to fear and never went back to sleep?

*

Time drives the flocks from field to fold,
When Rivers rage and Rocks grow cold,
And Philomel becometh dumb,
The rest complains of cares to come—

At some point, the nightingale falls silent. Time erases the song by numbing the wound, replacing it with fresh complaints: new hurts the singer can't yet fathom.
Sir Walter Ralegh, "The Nymph's Reply to the Shepherd," 5–8

*

I'd like to imagine that the fact I fought was the reason the attack ended, but the truth is he let me go. If he'd wanted more, there was no question *more* would have happened. I would have stopped fighting and become what some might call an accomplice to the act. I was, in fact, already going limp, subtly acceding to his desires in the hopes that, having satisfied them, he would stop. Perhaps this is why he pushed himself away. Perhaps it was enough that he'd grabbed and inserted and taken what he could within narrow legal, or personal, limits to prove a point to me and to himself: anything he wanted he could have. In the end, I was not so much a body to be reckoned with but a structure he would humiliate and dismantle.

*

In life, time's passage allows us to see ourselves change, but a poem's chronology forces us to see repetition: lyric time is not progressive but fragmentary and recursive. Traumatic time works like lyric time: the *now* of terror repeatedly breaking back through the crust of one's consciousness. Mourning the wound becomes an obsessive love of the lost. Mourning is merely the process by which we remain frozen: the birds always in flight, the hoopoe continually in pursuit. O, could our mourning ease thy misery!
Titus Andronicus, II, iv

*

One fantasy, in and outside of poetry, is that time itself stops. But Ralegh's point is that time never stops. Instead, its continual unfolding disorders memory, it blunts and numbs. Time is the subject that finally silences Philomela.

*

Compassion and retributive justice require that we hold multiple senses of time alive in mind: the past event, a punishment's present, the future in which this crime cannot or will no longer be enacted. Compassion calls for complex responses where vengeance calls for only one: a raving.

I don't have compassion for my attacker, just as I don't have a word for that day, only a description of its unfolding. Behind these descriptions, you may imagine the word or punishment you think appropriate. This act is done for yourself. It is not, though you may believe it is, at all useful to me.

*

Lucky, I think after he leaves, my shirt torn, nose running. Nothing stirs in the woods. Still I sit on the forest floor, unsure where to run. Will he come back? Will he be on the trail, will I see him in town? At the thought of town, at the thought of being seen by him or any other human, I shake and burn with shame.

*

I suspect it helped, not knowing what to call what happened in the woods. Not having the word, or refusing a word, forced me to imagine my own, allowed me both the privacy of my grief and the invention of private rituals to heal this grief. Keeping my attack secret also shielded me from the very real possibility of being called a hysteric. In that sense, silence protected me. Would I have grieved differently if someone had given me a legal term, a support group, a brochure?

Over time, shame and rage have abated. But not the memory. And not, at times, the overwhelming certainty that one day soon I will not be lucky again.

*

The nightingale hovers between trauma and memory, its song meant to
bring one into concert with the other, to integrate event into narrative, to
bring pain out of the body and into language. But the song isn't heard, it's
longed for. "Heard melodies are sweet," Keats writes, "but those unheard
/ are sweeter." The healing voice of the nightingale is only beautiful when
lodged in the imagination ("Jug jug," Eliot croons). The song stops, the
nightingale dies, and once more we descend into silence.
Keats, "Ode on a Grecian Urn," 11-12
T.S. Eliot, "The Waste Land," II, 27

*

Sappho saw the nightingale as a messenger of springtime and renewal.
Pliny the Elder said the bird could sing more than one song; nightingales
engage in singing contests, their songs changing over time. The song,
then, is not generic but individualized, depending on the hour of day and
also on the season. In poetry, the song may be one of suffering and loss;
in nature, it is simply one of life.
Pliny the Elder, *Historia Naturalis*, Book 10, Chapter 43

*

Does the bird sing or does it not sing? Is it a symbol for what threatens
to overwhelm our senses or for what permanently transforms? The bird
is death. No wonder Keats imagines himself dying when he hears it. No
wonder he scratches out the speech of Lavinia's tormentors in his copy
of Shakespeare: silence will come for him, as well as for her, and for all of
us. There is no shame in it. Death attends our longing for the song. Sing,
for you are voiceless. Sing, for it cannot matter. Sing, for soon no one will
hear you again.

*

I have spent my life devoted to an art whose foundational symbol is one of unspeakable violence. Did I seek poetry out for this? Or was I, that day in the woods, made into a poet? Perhaps, whether we are changed into our opposites or shrunk into the form that best defines us, some part of transformation is always a curse. *I am what I always was.* Perhaps it is sentimental to suggest violence has given me meaning, that the heart of poetry was only silence. Madness to say, yes, there's pain, but would I have changed without it?

*

If the song is beautiful, you will listen. In the field one day outside the residency, I encounter, or think I encounter, the bird that's charmed the opera singer. I am near a row of acacia trees when I hear its sudden, piercing trill of notes rise and fall. It could be any kind of bird, really, any kind of song. A cry of sex or terror, a mimicry of its parents or an invention all its own. A flourish it will teach to its offspring, its own embellishments branching through the ancient notes. It is the sound of time. It is the sound of time passing.

*

I stand in the field. I whistle back.

III

Quiver

after Carl Phillips

What do we do
        with memory, do we burn
or do we embellish it, do we
        study it as we do the elk

projected onto the archery
        studio screen, summer's
gelatin halo shivering
        between the antlers, replayed

whether or not
        anyone will come
to practice on or witness it: is this
        what memory is:

static, unchangeable
        mind we step into
and the clearing opens: again,
        light rain, the scent

of moss, puffs of steam
        rising off the slick,
black muzzle? Does the image,
        over time, brighten

so feverishly inside us,
        tearing through
the eye, the mind, the body: is it we
        who wander out now, tentative,

into late morning light?
        What does it mean
to forget so much,
        happily, greedily, if not

that we are nourished most
        on loss? The video
spools, the elk steps into
        then out of its field;

who cares, it was dead
        the second the camera
found it anyway, captured
        and projected endlessly

so that we might practice making it
        dead again.
Is this the image to convince you
        of the blinding

limits to our world?
        Is this another entry
to your newest opening?
        The animal turns, the screen

inside its body shakes:
        open, bright, pocked
by tips of arrows
        that never find their mark.

Gokstadt/Ganymede

In memoriam X, 1969–2016

In this obituary your wife, now widow,
posts, I find a photo of you running a hand
along *Gokstadt*'s blackened bow,
mizzen snapped, the nail bolts sanded
down by time. The photo could have been my own:
the same milk light dousing this Oslo hall
we separately visited, each drawn here alone
by myths we'd studied together in school.
Now the ship's grounded in perpetuity, hoisted
onto beetle-leg pylons. Night's maw. King's casket.
I study your face as you peer at a joist:
one plank jutting just out of concert, forever
a flaw, its weathered woods shellacked
and splayed, never to be smoothed back together.

Not odd, they'd said of your cousin, *just shy.*
All summer, he shadowed you, huge
in the cabin's outhouse doorway where you
hunched, a child unable to escape his hands,
one cinder-block palm smothering your cries—

After which you returned silent, wild-eyed
to your grandmother's couch. You grew
to resemble him, your broad back straining
your T-shirts. How you hated your body
in the pictures you showed me, eyes screwed
tight against the sun, tiny beside your cousin
bearing down on you as he fumbled with a shoe,
your smiling grandparents, the Kobuk's
black waters slapping a sun-bleached dock.

You never told. Vowels dissolved inside the walls
of other vowels: a labyrinth of sound
from which a boy would have to spool
out thread to escape. Pain's underground
of sense: shadowy maze where all language
is inadequate. What could you have said?
And how, explaining, would you have enlivened
that scene and self you most hated, imagined
them again by the force of saying it aloud?
To thrust yourself back into those hands, the cousin
clawing at his belt, that almost-human screech
to the screen door slamming behind you at the cabin—
Where, above the tree line, bristling and stark,
an owl cries, quartering, hunting the dark.

Fear of sex made you fear me. That look
you shot, after the film where the actress shies,
asked if she mistrusts her lover. The shook
head, the lie only I caught in the tilt of her eyes.
"No," she said—

                        It enraged you when I saw
what you didn't, worried one night I'd turn
and insist you'd hurt me. My body with its small,
waiting betrayals you could not fathom,
my sex you saw as a trap, which I did not
despise in you but pitied: the muscled weight
you shouldered into, that bulk you learned to carry
like your cousin, I said once, ignorant
of resemblance's meaning, why so suddenly
you'd recoil from me, flinching as if struck.

Once, fixing our car's engine, the white hood slipped
and your shoulder took its brunt, hunched
to catch the metal's glinting hinge, to stop
what would have snapped my wrist
in half, your quickness like that of a hawk's
launched at a rattler's coiling length.
The bruise I watched rise those days
along your shoulder blade: livid, a chalk-
yellow fringed with green like the rind
on a peach's blooming pink. Then that meaty
purple, rich as plums: a damson stain wine-
dark and velvet I put my mouth to, to taste
your skin's heat, your blood so close as to come
up throbbing through my tongue.

In dreams, someone calls me in the woods.
But when I turn it isn't you, just the pocked
face of a stranger, shirt and breath gin-soured,
body a grunting weight that knocks
the flight right out of me, pins me to the ground
when I try to run, one rough touch rooting
me in place. My limbs grow numb, bark-sheathed
and pale under the grasping fingers, shoots
of hair twined to hawthorn lances
that cut his knuckles, blood sprays
of winter berries spangling my branches
that he quickly hews away. *Something for me to keep,*
he says, or whispers, my own voice hissed away
into the wind's dull soughing of leaves.

And if I too had felt my head shoved
against shagged wood planks, scrubbed blood
from my thighs, or picked splinters
from my cheeks—? I could more than picture it,
my own violation making pain the place
our bodies might meet.

              The soft give of my breasts,
my rounded belly: these I offered up as gifts
to you, as if such frailty was what we'd share.
And when this failed to move you, whether
out of disgust or fear, I hardened myself to pure
muscle, starved away each craving till I pared
my way to a sleek essential: like you,
thin-hipped, raw-boned, indelible
to desire, and in that way, unassailable.

No. It wasn't our bodies but the word
you hated, *rape*'s crude distinctions
in which, except you confessed, you'd be seen
only as perpetrator, darkest sense in which
this word is harnessed to your sex.

Confess: another verb bound equally to both
criminal and victim, its barb attached to any
body, but lodged deepest in the wounds
of those you once dismissed to me as *weakest*.

For years, you wanted something masculine,
exclusive: terms no woman could lay claim to
or encompass within her experience.
Could never use to define you, who wouldn't live
with a language only I should know.

Out of the ship's hold they dug horses, hounds:
throats cut, buried to honor the king for whom
they hunted. Their bodies, like his own,
slashed and overmuscled—

                        Only the slender mound
of bones by his head now crowns him: shimmer
of blue, green, and gold eyes dappling his neck.
A peacock, sign he conquered worlds the kirk's
old chaplain, whose fields once housed him, never
saw. King of Norway, Egypt, India, his ancient
fist still clutches a brittle goblet saffron-
stained with the shape of a lion, its bloody yawn
cracked. A sovereign's glass skin transcending
flesh, time, and distance: his bones displayed in urns
turning him both mythic and familiar.

Two weeks, you messaged me. *Maybe four.*
Sudden November snows: freak storm
outside my window where light irradiates
each flake. The cancer returned not to your kidneys
but lungs. Forty-five years old: the same age
your father died. *Nature repeats itself,* you worried,
the oncologists screwing their metal crown
of gamma knifepoints into your brow, piercing
your scalp into a halo of wounds. You frown
for the photo your oldest friends, piecing
a life together, will later ponder: your face
iodined, bloated, as if your skull harbored
our grief, along with a parent's heritable illness.
Your body: was it ever yours alone?

In myths, we call it love. Call it desire
to soften the god who finds a boy, leads him
far from home, claps a cup in his hand, and demands
Bend to my will, child, you'll be adored—
To turn that god merely animal. To render
instinctual his greed, to make of him a man
barely culpable, so that we might command
a tale that only pleases us: there is no terror
in it, glossing over the sliced-out hole
in the family photos, the missing child
whose pain goes unremarked, silenced by a bolt
of lightning or the shriek of an eagle, its counter-
feit wings snatching a boy out of his life,
then making that boy serve him, forever.

As if a life could be defined by wound, sorrow
impelled only by desire—
                              I lay claim
to your private history, and by doing so chain
you once more to silence, my imagination
of your pain figured through my body, transforming
you to a self I might fathom. I wanted to mourn
how some do not survive so much as endure
what's forced on them, the heart's warm
muscle refreshed for the god that feeds
eternally on violence. Instead, I find myself
nursing the belief your wounds kept you
from hurting me. What you sensed, what I hated:
some part of me loved you, not in spite of,
but because you had been raped.

What will make these unearthed
fragments whole? Up close, the king's foramen
magnum is a sinkhole: nothing more than
variants where bone buckles, mimics Earth's
geologic shifts, its calcite scrapes

of shale, escarpments where the hair, a paste
of muds, has since flaked off. His cheek blades
are sheared to tusk tips. Broken by a spade
that crushed him where he lay,

he's shattered. A man to be returned in parts:
mined like a seam of crushed quartz, needles of bone
sharp as the points on a porcelain star.
So exposed when cleaned, arrayed, he almost glows
like the Dovre capped with a sugar-crust of snow.

Our first night, you pulled my dress
over my hips, tugging its green velvets
down. How I wish it was your mouth you'd let
be wetted with kisses: your shoulders pressed
to the bed, pearl lilies trapped behind glass.
Your rock-rose, pale flames
burning beneath my palm, you the tree
bursting into flower, you the bird
finally taking wing. I wish I could have made
our bodies one only of delight, never of suffering.
I wish that ivy dress had come softly twining
to our feet as we grafted ourselves into one
another: my slow blush ripening between us as
something in us both, finally, opened.

Somewhere grief's oceanic murmur sounds:
the faint snap of linen sails, or the prayers of mourners
hungry for ritual. I imagine your fingers
scrolling these hieroglyphs carved in rounds
through *Gokstadt*'s keel: an untranslatable lace
of beasts and love knots, maps of borders,
the king's own scrawled, brutal wars turned
quaint and historical. Their violence erased
by our disuse of such symbols, deadened
by the fact these words no longer represent us.
In time, I'll meet you here again: my ship's berth
swaddled in birch bark, stuffed with mosses.
Fragment from some mute, irredeemable past:
another mouth sewn closed against a tide of earth.

Telling the Wasps

It wasn't the bees I thought to tell but wasps
the evening you died. Not things that fly
from Earth to the underworld bearing sweetness
on their wings: grief made me bitter
and so in bitterness I went to seek
what roots among the mud and leaves, hanging
its home in ashes. I wanted to believe
this world would be our only one:
what other streams could run more cold,
what trees bloom with darker fruit?
I was happy here once, as were you.
I wanted to stay and grieve in the failing world
where we were human together.
And so I fell among the wasps, whispering
your name into the hole I scooped
beside the marshy winter creek, where wind
now scours the freezing water. Where reed
on broken reed hums its numb refrain,
and love turns in its mud home, and sleeps.

IV

Marsyas

We think Marsyas is the one
who changed, slipping from the forest
to challenge Apollo, staring at the god

he could never rival as if
into a harshly lit mirror, each recoiling

at what he found there: the jealousy knifed
inside the mortal talent, cold perfection
threaded through eternal rage.

But then the muses stirred behind them.
And Marsyas, out of the painful human wish
to be admired, cannot help but play.

And afterward, the cutting,
the stripped corpuscles, the ruined mouth—

      Only after his victory would Apollo reach out
and clip three small muscles from the satyr's throat
and shoulders, and dry them on a rock, and string them between
the curved horns of his lyre. Then the god

would pull a song
through that tender sinew, telling himself

it was not the crying of one
who has lost everything he loves but the god's
own singing that he heard, and after which
the muses strained because it was the song

of someone who knew what it was like
to be alive, which the god could not bear
to know, or to stop playing.

And so Apollo, unthinking, binds himself
to Marsyas: the god taking from his rival

fear and desire, the satyr hardened by the god's
cruel skill, until both songs
writhe inside each other, sung
by one who cannot understand death, and so

never understands what he plays,
knowing only how his hand
trembles over the plucked muscle:

adding, he thinks, something lower to the notes,
something sweeter, and infinitely strange.

Pasiphaë

So after M died, she turned
to the dog. His copper eyes, the sinewy
haunch muscles. The way he perched
by the door of M's study as if
sensing the body he missed
behind it. Something she would not
let herself feel, dry-eyed
at the funeral, refusing to gather
up the pants that still hung in his closet
beneath which the dog slept, breathing in
M's last particles until,
out of some extravagant kindness
or pity, she gave the dog
one of his sweaters. She watched
as the dog circled and pawed at it, tearing
at the tissuey material in his attempts
to fall asleep. *Impossible*
not to love such need, she thought, telling herself
it was this passion to come as close
as possible to what he'd never possess
that attracted her: she could not stop
touching him, pulling him
to her, gathering up the thick folds
of neck skin between her fingers, kneading
into her palms the hot popcorn smell
of his feet, his ears. Waking
in bed to a misty smear spread
across her sheets, red welts on her chest
from where he scratched and bit her.
She wanted to make the dog feel
for her some part of what was powerful
about his grief for M. She even began
to hate M's things, the cashmere sweater

now tossed in the trash, books and pants
burned, pictures of him swept
off the bedroom shelf. *Grief,*
her mother said, when she came to visit,
excusing her daughter's furious
disposals. *Though be careful you don't*
lose control of yourself, she warned,
as if too much feeling must be
a diminishment. The same lecture
she'd been given in high school
the night a boy came hours
late for a date, and still she ran,
uncomplainingly, to meet him. *Aren't you*
ashamed of yourself, her mother had said
upon her return, meaning
how willingly she had let herself
be debased. But love was a debasement.
In their first few months of courtship, M
had liked to crawl at her feet
during sex, eating the crackers
she held out as communion wafers, dressed
in the priest's black chasuble
he'd found for them: some nightmare-
colored sheath he'd scared up
from a local theater closet.
And she'd indulged him: their marriage,
their sex, she couldn't help it,
even when he asked her
to beat him, she did it: she'd never seen
anyone want something so nakedly before.

Three months after M's death, the dog
got fleas. And she watched him, mesmerized,
scratch at the thin skin of his ears, biting
at his legs and belly until they bled,
until she too let herself become

infested with them: her clothes, her sheets
speckled with the fat black pinheads
feasting on them both, the blood they shared
raising welts over her ribs. *One body,*
M once said as they lay, tangled
together, her legs pressed between his—
or was it his between hers?—their long limbs
muscular and bare, covered in the late
afternoon light with the same
fine gold furze of hair. How close she'd come
to really loving him. *You must get rid*
of that animal, her mother declared
one night at the kitchen table, horrified
by her necklace of bites, her wolfish
eating habits. How greedily
she ate: the sad result, her mother said,
of living too long alone. *You're little*
better than that dog, her mother scolded her,
at which point she rose from the table,
tossed her food to the floor,
and got down on all fours to eat it.

The Olive Tree at Vouves

> His shoots will sprout and his beauty will be unto the
> olive tree—
>> Hosea 14:6

To write
about the tree is not
        to write about the human, and yet
        to see this olive

split in two—or is it
two trees woven
        into one—sinuous,
        long-backed—is to think

of a man's thigh
wound around another's, hip
        to hip joined
        at the silver bole

of bark that smells
of sun and the dark oils
        of scalp and groin, a mouth of water
        shared by beings

both apart from and inside of
each other. Once
        I saw a man take another
        like this among the shadowed

pines outside the museum where
everyone knew
        men went. To hide
        or not as was their wont

those days in the city when they said
the men were dying and we
             should raze the grove to keep
             them out. Who knew

what wind, what soil
might carry? Who knows
             why I see these men
             again here, brief flare

of fear and desire resurrected
in this bark, another life I can have
             no knowledge of except
             by what the tree

suggests and memory—
sterile, fading—dissolves into.
             The olive tree of Vouves
             has been alive

two thousand years. Olives,
it seems, do not have
             to die: shoots split
             the elder's center, feed

within its roots, taking from it
form, nutrient, light; taking from it
             skin and weather until
             the thorn crowns shake,

lustrous, indifferent
beside it. But I
             am not talking about the human
             here: not myth, not lovers,

not even a man
lingering in a grove at night,
        waiting for a friend to find
        or betray him. Only olives

shivering in their winter
silvers. How solitary
        they seem like this, raw-
        skinned, taut:

their embrace
so like our own
        though I know
        it is not.

Driving to Santa Fe

Quick swim up
through the headlights: gold eye
a startle in black: green, swift glance
raking mine. A full second
we held each other, gone.
Gone. And how did I know
what to call it? *Lynx,* the only possible
reply though I'd never seen one. The car
filling with it: moonlight,
piñon: a cat's acrid smell
of terror. How quickly the gray body
fled, swerving to avoid
my light. And how often
that sight returns to me, shames me
to know how much more this fragment
matters. More than the broad back
of a man I loved. More than the image
of my friend, cancer-struck, curled
beside her toilet. More than my regret
for the child I did not have, which I thought
once would pierce me utterly. Nothing
beside that dense muscle, faint gold guard hairs
stirring the dark. And if I keep
these scraps of it, what did it keep of me?
A flight, a thunder. A shield of light
dropped before the eyes, pinned
inside that magnificent skull only time
would release. Split back, fade
and reveal. Wind
would open him. Sun would turn him
commonplace: a knot of flies, a ribcage
of shredded tendon, wasp-nest
fragile. The treasure of him, like anything,

gone. Even now, I thumb that face
like a coin I cannot spend. If something in me
ever lived, it lived in him, fishing the cold
trout-thick streams, waking to snow, dying
when he died, which is a comfort.
I must say this. Otherwise, I myself
do not exist. It looked at me
a moment. A flash of green, of gold
and white. Then the dark came down again
between us. Once, I was afraid
of being changed. Now that is finished.
The lynx has me in its eye.
I am already diminished.

Pear

after Susan Stewart

No one ever died for a bite
of one, or came back from the dead
for a single taste: the cool flesh
cellular or stony, white

as the belly of the winter hare
or a doe's scut, flicking,
before she mates. Even an unripe one

is delicious, its crisp bite cleaner
almost than water and its many names
just as inviting: Bartlett and Comice,

Anjou, Nashi, Concorde
and Seckel, the pomegranate-skinned
Starkrimson, even the medieval

Bosc, which looks like it dropped
from an oil painting. It is not a sin
to eat one, though you may think

of a woman's body as you do it,
the bell-shaped swell of it
rich in your hand, and for this reason

it was sacred to Venus, Juno, all women
celebrated or dismissed
in its shape, that mealy sweetness
tunneling from its center, a gold

that sinks back into itself with age.
To ripen a pear, wrap it in paper,
lay it in cloth by an open window

or slip a rotten one beside it
on a metal dish: dying cells call always
to the fresh ones, the body's

siren song that, having heard
it once, we can't stop singing.
This is not the fruit

that will send you to hell
nor keep you there;
it will not give you knowledge,

childbirth, power, or love:
you won't know more pain
for having eaten one, or choke
on a bite to fall asleep

under glass. It has no use
for archer or hero, though
anything you desire from an apple

you can do with the pear, like a dark sister
with whom you might live out
your secret desires. Cook it

in wine, mull it with spices, roast it
with honey and cloves. Time sweetens
and we taste it, so gather the fruit

weeks before ripeness,
let summer and winter both
simmer inside, for it is

a fall fruit whose name in China
means separation, though only the fearful
won't eat one with those they love.

To grow a tree from seed,
you'll need a garden
and a grafting quince, bees, a ladder,

shears, a jug; you'll need water
and patience, sun and mud,
a reverence for the elders

who told no true stories
of this fruit's origin,
wanting to give us the freedom
of one thing that's pleasure alone.

Cool and sweet, cellular and stony,
this is the fruit I'll never die for,
nor come back from the dead

for a single taste.
The juice of the pear
shines on my cheeks.

There is no curse in it. I'll eat
what I like and throw the rest
to the grasses. The seeds

will find whatever soils they were meant for.

Pythagorean

Arguing, in answer to the joking
question posed by their dinner's host,
that humankind's distinguishing feature
must be empathy, the young lawyer finds himself
thinking suddenly of his mother.
A poor woman, not in money, as he would tell
his friends, but kindness, she raised him
and his brother during the two
lost decades she spent struggling
with alcoholism. Which kept him sober
through his twenties, until DC,
where on a dare one night
he went to a hotel bar to order
Jameson after Jameson whiskey, neat: curiosity
having finally compelled him to see
if he might feel some part of his mother's
deep, sweet craving take root in him; some
heritable need that might make him feel
sympathy for her who once, drunk and in a rage,
broke his five-year-old brother's arm.
It was almost disappointing to see
how easily he could push away
the drink; as disappointing as when he'd learned
his mother only stopped when a doctor
said she had to, not out of any love
for her children but out of terror
for herself, retaining to the last,
he thought, an essential selfishness. Empathy
was not the starting point of change
for her but fear: sobriety seemed only
to clarify an essential indifference
she must have felt for them, whetting the knife's
edge of her later self-pity, just as he found his own

disinterest in drink made him feel
both less forgiving toward his mother
and more alone. *We can't anticipate*
our effect on others, because we cannot read
all the data that surround us, argues
the mathematician now, interrupting
the lawyer's thoughts, as he lists for the table
all the usual horrors: landfills, oil leaks
in the Gulf of Mexico, California either flooding
or out of water. *We exist only*
in the data, he continues, *numbers*
inside a formula that's constantly changing:
the whole thing moving together
like a flock of starlings, he finishes, glancing
at the literature professor across from him to see
how she has taken this flourish. His wife,
a doctor, notices; notices also the woman's
black hair, her olive skin, for a moment,
annoyed by her husband's clumsiness
in flirting with her. She herself can easily picture
the image he's recounted, coming as it has
from their life together, the dawn they spent
on a birding tour he'd taken her on
for their anniversary. Her husband
had been captivated by the thought
of witnessing a murmuration, and so they'd stood
all dawn in a wet field to watch
swarms of birds stretch
and collapse above them in dark parabolas,
one shape lifting out of the next, blooming
and rising without once
seeming to collide. *It must be sex*
that drives them to it, she remembers
teasing her husband, though she regrets
having said this, it had diminished

the morning, her husband's joy, the whirling,
star-shaped arms glittering above them.
Perhaps, she thinks, looking
at the young professor, this woman
would have been more moved.
She imagines the other woman
there now in the field, softening
under her husband's attention. She imagines her
taking his hand. She imagines her following him
into their host's marble bathroom,
pressing against him by the onyx sink.
Now the two of them are alone
at her own home while she's at work:
her husband has just finished an article;
the literature professor, who lives
nearby, has wandered over
with a cup of coffee. It would be easy for her
to do this: to take off her blouse, her shoes,
her skirt, to offer herself to him, so young
he could never refuse her, the doctor
flushing now, thinking of it, bemused
by this jealousy that she alone
has authored. Perhaps this
is the defining feature of humanity,
she thinks: the capacity to imagine
some small cruelty and take pleasure in it,
regardless of the truth, knowing later
she won't be able to stop herself
from punishing her husband. The young
literature professor, a recent
transplant from Lahore, has been texting
all night beneath the dinner table.
She's comforting her son, who's asked to leave
the expensive boarding school
she enrolled him in after the bomb

ripped through the concert hall they'd nearly
visited together. He wants to join her
in America, he says. He's sick
of the food, the rules, and she is lying to him,
promising he'll come join her in the US soon
after winter break, though she won't
ever let him. If it is dangerous at home
it is dangerous here, too: she does not want
him to become like her students, his brash
yet strangely sensitive temperament crystallizing
unchecked in the American classroom,
his haphazard talent for work turned
into a satisfaction with his own ignorance.
She has no patience for this, for the man
sitting beside her now at the table, moving his arms
in slow, fluid motions, *like a dancer,* she thinks,
but not in a way meant to compliment him,
repulsed by his strange, plump hands,
the sharp looks he still manages to draw
from his doctor wife. She can see that he is drunk,
like the smooth-cheeked lawyer beside him,
and that, careless with his looks, he is trying
to impress her, and he is—she reminds him
of a woman he once dated in college: the same
shrewd, unamused expressions
darkening her face. Which is why
he'd thought of the starlings at all
this evening, and why he has grown
somewhat morose now recalling them, the plans
he'd made to take his college girlfriend
on the birding tour for her birthday. Something
she on her own would never have done, calling it
frivolous, moved, if at all, by the sight, only
by what she would have called the birds'
fractal intelligence. She

a disciple of Pythagoras, as he used to tease her,
because she studied geometry, because she liked
to insist the world was one vicious being
devouring another, their own attraction determined
only by their proximity to each other, a connection
that felt safer to her than love, an idea
which strikes him now as a truthful
distillation of their relationship
that also demeaned it. Which is why
he is relieved it was his wife in the end
he took to watch the birds, their scattershot rise
from a stand of beech trees. How solid
they'd seemed, skimming the treetops
in long scarves, constellatory arms. *They feel*
their way into it, the guide had told them,
and his wife shivered against his shoulder.
So many dark wings beating the air. Uncountable,
though every year there were fewer. His girlfriend
never finished college because she died,
struck by a car on one of her runs. The birds
would have frightened her, he knew,
their sudden dips and changes, their great
chattering cries that became, over minutes,
unbearable. He'd had to cup his hands
over his ears to mute them. Did he ever see
them land? he wonders. They must have settled,
but had he seen them do it? He remembers
only that the skies had cleared a moment, the birds
thinning as they separated from one another.
How calm he'd felt, as his wife reached for his hand.
And then they were up again, and flowing, and flown.

Paisley Rekdal is the author of three works of nonfiction and five previous books of poetry, including *Animal Eye,* which won the 2013 UNT Rilke Prize and was a finalist for the 2013 Kingsley Tufts Poetry Award, and *Imaginary Vessels,* which was a finalist for the 2018 Kingsley Tufts Poetry Award. Her work has appeared in *The American Poetry Review, The New Republic,* the *New York Times Magazine, Poetry, Tin House,* and five editions of *The Best American Poetry* series, among other publications. A former Guggenheim fellow and NEA recipient, in 2017 she was elected Utah's poet laureate.

Poetry is vital to language and living. Since 1972, Copper Canyon Press has published extraordinary poetry from around the world to engage the imaginations and intellects of readers, writers, booksellers, librarians, teachers, students, and donors.

WE ARE GRATEFUL FOR THE MAJOR SUPPORT PROVIDED BY:

THE PAUL G. ALLEN
FAMILY FOUNDATION

CULTURE

Lannan

Anonymous (3)

Jill Baker and Jeffrey Bishop

Anne and Geoffrey Barker

Donna and Matt Bellew

John Branch

Diana Broze

The Beatrice R. and Joseph A. Coleman
Foundation, Inc.

Laurie and Oskar Eustis

Mimi Gardner Gates

Nancy Gifford

Gull Industries, Inc. on behalf of
William True

The Trust of Warren A. Gummow

Petunia Charitable Fund and advisor
Elizabeth Hebert

Bruce Kahn

Phil Kovacevich and Eric Wechsler

Lakeside Industries, Inc. on behalf of
Jeanne Marie Lee

Maureen Lee and Mark Busto

Rhoady Lee and Alan Gartenhaus

Peter Lewis

Ellie Mathews and Carl Youngmann as
The North Press

Hank Meijer

Gregg Orr

Gay Phinny

Suzie Rapp and Mark Hamilton

Emily and Dan Raymond

Jill and Bill Ruckelshaus

Kim and Jeff Seely

Richard Swank

Dan Waggoner

Barbara and Charles Wright

Caleb Young as C. Young Creative

The dedicated interns and faithful
volunteers of Copper Canyon Press

TO LEARN MORE ABOUT UNDERWRITING COPPER CANYON PRESS TITLES,
PLEASE CALL 360-385-4925 EXT. 103

Lannan Literary Selections

For two decades Lannan Foundation has supported the publication and distribution of exceptional literary works. Copper Canyon Press gratefully acknowledges their support.

LANNAN LITERARY SELECTIONS 2019

Jericho Brown, *The Tradition*

Deborah Landau, *Soft Targets*

Paisley Rekdal, *Nightingale*

Natalie Scenters-Zapico, *Lima :: Limón*

Matthew Zapruder, *Father's Day*

RECENT LANNAN LITERARY SELECTIONS FROM
COPPER CANYON PRESS

Sherwin Bitsui, *Dissolve*

Marianne Boruch, *Cadaver, Speak*

John Freeman, *Maps*

Jenny George, *The Dream of Reason*

Ha Jin, *A Distant Center*

Deborah Landau, *The Uses of the Body*

Maurice Manning, *One Man's Dark*

Rachel McKibbens, *blud*

W. S. Merwin, *The Lice*

Aimee Nezhukumatathil, *Oceanic*

Camille Rankine, *Incorrect Merciful Impulses*

Paisley Rekdal, *Imaginary Vessels*

Brenda Shaughnessy, *So Much Synth*

Frank Stanford, *What About This: Collected Poems of Frank Stanford*

Ocean Vuong, *Night Sky with Exit Wounds*

C. D. Wright, *Casting Deep Shade*

Javier Zamora, *Unaccompanied*

Ghassan Zaqtan (translated by Fady Joudah), *The Silence That Remains*

The Chinese character for poetry is made up of two parts:
"word" and "temple." It also serves as pressmark for
Copper Canyon Press.

The poems are set Minion Pro.
Book design and composition by Phil Kovacevich.